JANUARY

Ellen Jackson

Illustrated by
Pat DeWitt and Robin DeWitt

Charlesbridge

*To my dear friend
Carmel Robertson
—E. J.*

*To Jean Diggs for all your
support and friendship and
in loving memory of our
aunt, Patricia Gouse
—P. D. & R. D.*

Did You Know?

January is a month of new beginnings. People welcome the new year with parties and parades, fireworks and fun.

Jack Frost, an imaginary elf, is a symbol of this time of year. The delicate patterns of frost on trees and windows are said to be samples of his work.

There are several superstitions about the first day of January. One says that doors and windows must be opened to let the new year in and the old year out. Another superstition forbids sweeping and dusting so that good luck is not swept away.

January is the first full month of winter in the Northern Hemisphere. The Japanese poet Shiki described the icy beauty of a winter day in this haiku:

> *First snow last night . . .*
> *there across the morning bay*
> *sudden mountain—white*

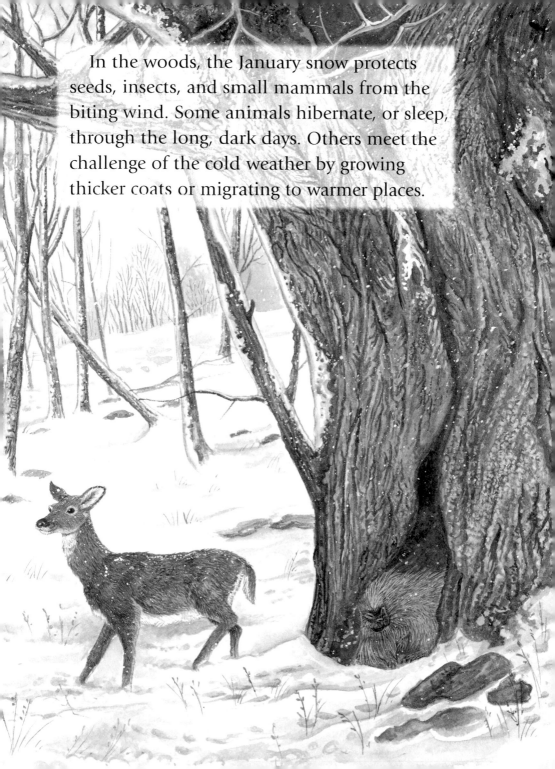

In the woods, the January snow protects seeds, insects, and small mammals from the biting wind. Some animals hibernate, or sleep, through the long, dark days. Others meet the challenge of the cold weather by growing thicker coats or migrating to warmer places.

In northern cities, a big snowstorm leaves the roads heaped with snow. Highways are blocked off, water pipes freeze, and power lines go down. After the storm, children build snowmen or have snowball fights in the fresh, new snow.

Many people go snowboarding, sledding, or skiing in January. It is exciting to rush down a steep slope and feel the crisp tingle of cold air on your face. Champion skiers often come from places with cold climates such as the United States or Canada. Children in these countries even ski to school.

In some parts of the United States, the winter weather is warm and balmy. In Hawaii, people can enjoy surfing, waterskiing, and canoeing in January. In southern California, people play beach volleyball throughout the winter months.

Volleyball can be played indoors as well as outdoors, so it is a great winter activity in any weather. In this fast-paced sport, players jump into the air to pass, block, or spike the ball. Volleyball is one of the few sports where girls and boys often play on the same team.

The January Birthstone

The birthstone for January is the garnet, a beautiful crystal that comes in many colors, including red, violet, green, and cinnamon. Garnets can be found in more than one hundred different places in the United States. They are also found in Central Europe, Russia, and South Africa.

In the Middle Ages, garnets were said to protect those who wore them from bad dreams. A particularly beautiful red garnet as large as a hen's egg is displayed in the Vienna Museum in Austria.

The January Flower

If you were born in January, your special
flower is the carnation. Carnations have been
grown for more than two thousand years. In
the thirteenth century, crusaders who became
sick with the plague drank wine mixed with
carnation leaves to help control their fevers.
Today Hawaiian leis, or garlands, are often
made of carnations.

The January Zodiac

Capricorn, the goat, is the astrological sign for people with birthdays from December 22 to January 19. People born under Capricorn are thought to like regular schedules and have a place for everything. They enjoy their homes and have a few close friends. A Capricorn cannot be bossed around and likes to go his or her own way.

The sign for people born from January 20 to February 18 is Aquarius, the water carrier. Those born under Aquarius are able to see both sides of an argument. They are good judges of other people. They love nature and are talented in astronomy, science, history, photography, and anything concerned with electricity. But an Aquarius can sometimes daydream a little too much.

The Calendar

January is the first month of the year and has thirty-one days. In the early days of Rome, the new year began in March, and January had only thirty days. At a later time, the Roman calendar was changed, and January became the first month of the year. In 46 B.C., Julius Caesar added a day to January, giving it thirty-one days, its present number.

The Romans named January after Janus, the god of beginnings and endings. Janus is always shown with two heads because the Romans believed he could look into the future as well as the past.

Sun, Sky, and Weather

In the woodlands, a frozen lake groans and cracks as it shrinks and expands with the changing temperature. When the sun shines, ice crystals dazzle the eye.

January is a good month for learning about snow. Put a piece of black cloth in the freezer until it is frozen stiff. Then take it outside, catch some snowflakes on the cloth, and examine them with a magnifying glass.

In the late 1800s, a man named Wilson Bentley took more than six thousand photographs of snowflakes. His photographs showed that no two snowflakes are exactly the same.

January weather can also be sunny, mild, and dry. In parts of Texas, winter is the driest season of the year. Temperatures in Death Valley, California, average sixty degrees Fahrenheit during the day, and rain is so rare that footprints left in the soil can last for years.

The January full moon has been called the wolf moon by some Native American peoples of the Northeast. The Anglo-Saxons, who settled in Britain in the fifth and sixth centuries, called January *Wulf monath*, or wolf month. This is probably because in January, packs of hungry wolves looking for food sometimes approached human settlements.

Animals in January

In the woods, blue jays and finches hunt for seeds, acorns, and berries. Ducks sit on the ice of a frozen pond. A layer of fat beneath their feathers keeps them warm.

The winter snow helps some small mammals survive. One inch of snow is enough to hide mice from predators. The snow piles help cottontail rabbits reach the buds on saplings. The deeper the snow, the higher the rabbits can reach.

People in some parts of the United States, such as the Florida Everglades, seldom see frost and snow. In January, when the Everglades marshes begin to dry out, alligators scoop out plants and mud to create "gator" holes. The holes gradually fill with underground water, attracting raccoons, otters, storks, turtles, and snails. These animals find food and water at the gator holes, and some of them, in turn, become food for the alligators.

In California, brown pelicans begin breeding in January. The adults dive for fish from thirty feet above the ocean's surface. The force of the dive stuns the fish so the pelicans can catch them.

Gray whales spend their summers in the cold waters of the Arctic, but by January, you can see them swimming along the Pacific Coast on their way to Baja California. As many as two hundred whales may pass within a mile of Point Reyes National Seashore in the first two weeks of January. An adult gray whale can weigh as much as ten elephants and be as long as a bus.

In the desert, life goes on as usual for many animals—but not for all. In January, the poorwill, the only bird known to hibernate, finds a cozy spot on a rocky cliff or inside the trunk of a dead cactus plant and falls into a deep sleep that may last for months. People have actually picked up the sleeping bird without waking it.

The spotted skunk, the smallest skunk in the United States, also lives in the Southwest. It does not hibernate, but during January, it spends more time napping and resting in its burrow. Occasionally it goes out to hunt for mice or other small animals.

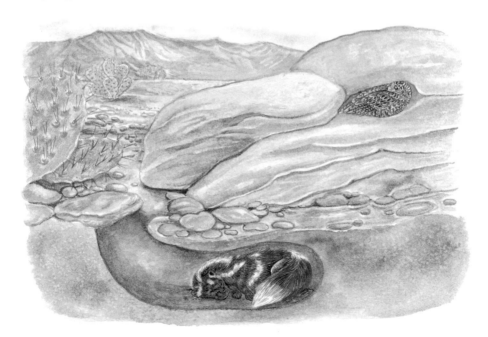

Plants in January

In the northern woods, heavy snow bends the branches of the birch trees to the ground. The trees spring back up when the snow melts or falls off. If the storm lasts several days, however, the trees may never completely recover.

Have you ever wondered what animals eat in the winter? If you look closely, you will see that some berries, pinecones, apples, and dry seed heads left over from autumn still cling to plants and trees. They provide food for birds and mammals.

Many plants appear dead and dry in the winter, but the stalks of some are alive, and animals can browse on these. The evening primrose produces a winter fruit and rows of loose seeds that look like coffee grounds. Sometimes insects spend the winter in the seed cases.

Winter in southern Florida is warm and mild. In January, saw grass, a plant that covers thousands of square miles in the Everglades, turns gold and withers in the sun.

A plant with large leaves called an alligator flag grows around the edges of gator holes. Hunters once used this plant as a sign that alligators were nearby.

Creosote, the most common shrub in North America, still has green leaves. Desert shrubs like creosote spread their roots over large areas to collect enough rainwater to live. One creosote bush called King Clone grows in the Mojave Desert and is about ten thousand years old. It is one of the oldest living things known.

Special Days

New Year's Day

In most of Europe and North America, the first day of January is the beginning of the new year. No one knows when or how people began to celebrate New Year's Day. Ancient clay tablets tell of one New Year's festival that took place three thousand years ago in Mesopotamia.

Today people welcome the new year with parties and celebrations. On New Year's Eve, friends and relatives gather together. On the stroke of midnight, everyone dances, sings, or shouts. People say good-bye to the past and hope for a new and better future. Some people make resolutions, or promises, to do things differently beginning on New Year's Day.

Martin Luther King Jr. Day

Martin Luther King Jr., born on January 15, 1929, is honored on the third Monday of January in the United States. Dr. King fought for the civil rights of African Americans by organizing demonstrations and making powerful speeches that stirred the hearts of people everywhere. In one speech, he said, "I have a dream that one day . . . little black boys and black girls will be able to join hands with little white boys and white girls as sisters and brothers."

Dr. King believed that people should disobey, in a nonviolent way, laws that were unjust. He thought that voting was the best way to change things.

On April 4, 1968, Dr. King was assassinated in Memphis, Tennessee. While many of his goals have been accomplished, much remains to be done.

Chinese New Year

The first day of the Chinese new year happens each year between January 21 and February 20. The exact date depends on the phase of the moon. Before the new year begins, each Chinese family honors the god of the kitchen, who is said to visit the emperor of Heaven during the last week of the old year. Feasting and fireworks are part of the festivities.

On New Year's Day, celebrations take place in the street. A huge paper dragon, propelled by people standing underneath it, dances to the music of drums. People hang money from doorways, and the dancers collect it as they go by. They use the money to help the community.

Famous January Events

On January 7, 1785, Dr. John Jeffries, a Boston doctor, and Jean-Pierre Blanchard, a French aeronaut, were the first to cross the English Channel in a hot-air balloon. The ride from Dover, England, to near Calais, France, was a bumpy one. To avoid landing in the ocean, the two men threw their equipment and most of their clothes overboard. Blanchard's trousers were the last item to go.

On the morning of January 24, 1848, gold was discovered on a California ranch owned by John Augustus Sutter. Soon trappers, farmers, sailors, lawyers, and others flocked to the area, hoping to strike it rich. While very few people found wealth, the gold rush brought thousands of people to northern California and helped establish San Francisco as a thriving city.

On January 1, 1863, Abraham Lincoln issued the Emancipation Proclamation. It freed African Americans from slavery in most parts of the South. From that day on, when Northern soldiers fighting in the Civil War occupied a region, they

gave the slaves their freedom. Many former slaves joined the Union Army and helped fight against their former masters.

On January 28, 1986, the tenth flight of the space shuttle *Challenger* ended tragically seventy-three seconds after liftoff. *Challenger* exploded, killing everyone on board, including Christa McAuliffe, a teacher who had been chosen to accompany the astronauts on the flight. As a result, many changes were made at NASA, the agency that oversees the United States space program.

Birthdays

Many famous people were born in January.

Betsy Ross

January 1, 1752

Creator of the first stars-and-stripes flag for the United States.

Louis Braille

January 4, 1809

Inventor of a system of reading and writing by touch for the blind.

Nancy Lopez Knight

January 6, 1957

American golfer and four-time winner of the Ladies Professional Golf Association Player-of-the-Year Award.

Elvis Presley

January 8, 1935

Popular American rock singer.

Albert Schweitzer

January 14, 1875

Philosopher, musician, physician, and winner of the 1952 Nobel Peace Prize.

Muhammad Ali

January 17, 1942

World heavyweight boxing champion.

Corazon Aquino

January 25, 1933

First woman president of the Philippines, who led her country toward greater freedom and democracy.

Wolfgang Amadeus Mozart

January 27, 1756

Musician and composer whose works include *The Magic Flute* and the *Jupiter* symphony.

Oprah Winfrey

January 29, 1954

TV talk show hostess, actress, and producer.

Franklin D. Roosevelt

January 30, 1882

Thirty-second president of the United States and the only president to serve more than two terms.

A January Story

The North Wind had three sons who were called White Feet, White Wings, and White Hands. When the world was new, these three sons came to the earth from their invisible palace. They moved across the land, transforming the world and everything in it.

But they were so beautiful that the people and animals could not bear to gaze at them. So White Feet, White Wings, and White Hands went far away beyond the Gates of the Sunset to talk to the North Wind. The North Wind listened to their story and blew upon them with his mighty breath.

When they returned through the Gates of Dawn, White Feet, White Wings, and White Hands were no longer visible to the children of the earth, nor have they been seen since.

But they are still among us, and in winter, you can see their handiwork. White Feet treads across the land and spreads a soft blanket over field and forest. Wherever he walks, a great silence falls upon the hills and valleys. White Wings ruffles the waves of the sea and sends clouds scurrying across the sky. And White Hands quiets the waterfall until it hangs like a curtain against the mountain.

We know them now only by their passing, and we call them snow, winter wind, and ice.

AUTHOR'S NOTE

This book gives an overview of the month of January in North America. But nature does not follow a strict schedule. The mating and migration of animals, the blooming of plants, and other natural events vary from year to year, or occur earlier or later in different places.

The zodiac sections of this book are included just for fun as part of the folklore of the month and should not be taken as accurate descriptions of any real people.

The January story was adapted from the archives of the Dalriada Celtic Heritage Society, Isle of Arran, Scotland.

Text copyright © 2002 by Ellen Jackson
Illustrations copyright © 2002
  by Pat DeWitt and Robin DeWitt
All rights reserved, including the right of
  reproduction in whole or in part in any form.
The illustration of Christa McAuliffe on page 27
  is based on a photograph courtesy of NASA.

Published by Charlesbridge Publishing
85 Main Street, Watertown, MA 02472
(617) 926-0329
www.charlesbridge.com

Illustrations done in watercolor on Arches
  hot-press paper
Display type and text type set in Giovanni
Color separations made by Sung In Printing,
  South Korea
Printed and bound by Sung In Printing,
  South Korea
Production supervision by Brian G. Walker
Designed by Diane M. Earley

**Library of Congress
Cataloging-in-Publication Data**

Jackson, Ellen B., 1943-
    January/Ellen Jackson; illustrated by
    Pat DeWitt and Robin DeWitt.
        p. cm.—(It happens in the month of)
    ISBN 0-88106-995-7 (hardcover)
    1. January—Folklore. 2. January—Juvenile
    literature. [1. January.] I. DeWitt, Pat, ill.
    II. DeWitt, Robin, ill. III. Title.

GR930.J334   2002
398'.33—dc21   2001028264

Printed in South Korea
10 9 8 7 6 5 4 3 2 1